Peeps at Many Lands

You are holding a reproduction of an original work that is in the public domain in the United States of America, and possibly other countries. You may freely copy and distribute this work as no entity (individual or corporate) has a copyright on the body of the work. This book may contain prior copyright references, and library stamps (as most of these works were scanned from library copies). These have been scanned and retained as part of the historical artifact.

This book may have occasional imperfections such as missing or blurred pages, poor pictures, errant marks, etc. that were either part of the original artifact, or were introduced by the scanning process. We believe this work is culturally important, and despite the imperfections, have elected to bring it back into print as part of our continuing commitment to the preservation of printed works worldwide. We appreciate your understanding of the imperfections in the preservation process, and hope you enjoy this valuable book.

PEEPS AT MANY LANDS
KOREA

BY
CONSTANCE J. D. COULSON

WITH TWELVE FULL-PAGE ILLUSTRATIONS
IN COLOUR
BY
THE AUTHOR AND E. H. FITCHEW

LONDON
ADAM AND CHARLES BLACK
1910

CONTENTS

CHAPTER		PAGE
I.	THE WOMEN AND CHILDREN	1
II.	KOREAN SUPERSTITIONS	11
III.	ABOUT GINSENG AND OTHER THINGS	17
IV.	A VISIT TO THE EMPEROR	21
V.	THE HISTORY OF THE PEOPLE	24
VI.	A JOURNEY TO PING YANG	29
VII.	THE CLOTHES OF THE KOREANS	35
VIII.	THE PEOPLE AND THEIR BELIEFS	40
IX.	A KOREAN HOUSE	43
X.	A KOREAN FAIRY-TALE	48
XI.	HOW EUROPEANS FIRST WENT TO KOREA	51
XII.	THE SIGHTS OF SEOUL	56
XIII.	THE FOUR ESTATES OF THE REALM	61
XIV.	A ROYAL PROCESSION	65
XV.	CONCERNING SEOUL	69
XVI.	THE HISTORY OF CHRISTIANITY IN KOREA	74
XVII.	A MORNING WALK	78
XVIII.	KOREA BECOMES PART OF THE JAPANESE EMPIRE UNDER ITS OLD NAME OF "CHOSEN"	83

LIST OF ILLUSTRATIONS

	ARTIST.	
KOREAN BOYS	Mrs. Coulson	Frontispiece
		FACING PAGE
PASS ON THE ROAD FROM SEOUL TO PEKING	E. H. Fitchew	viii
A KOREAN BRIDEGROOM	Mrs. Coulson	9
YOUNG MARRIED MAN	,,	16
MR. KIM KUI HAI, LATE INTERPRETER TO THE BRITISH LEGATION	,,	25
WASHER-WOMEN BY THE RIVERSIDE	E. H. Fitchew	32
KOREAN GIRL IN WINTER DRESS	Mrs. Coulson	41
MONUMENT WITH TORTOISE PEDESTAL IN THE PUBLIC GARDENS, SEOUL	E. H. Fitchew	48
LOTUS POND IN THE PALACE GARDENS, SEOUL	,,	57
ONE OF THE GATEWAYS ON THE CITY WALL, SEOUL	,,	64
SERVANTS OF THE EMPEROR	Mrs. Coulson	73
THE PEKING PASS	E. H. Fitchew	80

Map of Korea on page vii

MAP OF KOREA

KOREA

CHAPTER I

THE WOMEN AND CHILDREN

THE country of Korea, or, as the natives call it, Chosen (the Land of the Morning Calm), lies between China and Japan. It occupies a peninsula which juts out from Manchuria, and is bounded on one side by the Sea of Japan and on the other by the Yellow Sea. Since the Manchu Conquest in 1644 it has been a tributary State of the Chinese Empire until some ten years ago, when it threw off this allegiance and declared itself independent. Korea is a beautiful country, hilly and well wooded. A range of mountains called the Diamond Mountains, containing some high peaks, runs down almost the entire length of the eastern coast. Seoul, the capital, is the centre of everything, whether of business, pleasure, or of such culture as has found its way

Korea

into the "Hermit Kingdom." The Emperor never leaves the city; therefore all who wish to appeal to him for justice or mercy, or to obtain deliverance, must present themselves in Seoul. All round the city runs a high wall, which is wide enough for seven or eight people to walk abreast. The hills stand close round, and in several places the wall is carried over the slopes of these hills, so that parts of them are included in the city area. There are seven gates in the wall, which are closed every evening at sundown. The principal streets of Seoul are now wide and well kept, but until a few years ago they were uneven and full of great holes, and were usually crowded with little hovels and booths, which would be hurriedly cleared away whenever it was known that the Emperor would pass that way. Even now the authorities have to keep a very sharp lookout indeed, because quaint little huts of wattle and mud, about eight feet square, have a way of appearing in the thoroughfares, coming up like mushrooms in the course of a night. A family of half a dozen people will be quite happy in a house of these dimensions.

Children in Korea have a particularly good time. Their mothers indulge them, and provide them

The Women and Children

with the prettiest and brightest-coloured clothes they can afford to buy; and their fathers never look so happy as when they walk out with a little son or sons, for there is no denying that in Korea girls are not nearly so much appreciated as their brothers. Almost as soon as he can toddle the little boy is put into the dress of a man—full white trousers and white or coloured short coat; a longer coat is worn over this for smart occasions. The boy who is neither betrothed nor married wears his hair drawn back from the forehead and plaited into a long pigtail. Boys are married at any time after they have reached seven years, and from that age onwards are considered and treated as men. Their hair is then twisted into a knot on the top of their heads, and they wear a little hat of pale coarse straw perched jauntily above this. With their long coats, generally of blue or pink, these tiny bridegrooms swagger along, looking as proud as little turkey-cocks.

Korean girls have a very jolly time while they are small, playing about with their brothers, but when they are seven or eight this free life ceases for them. Henceforth they must keep within doors until they are married, and even then it is only women of the working classes who can

Korea

walk about freely. Korean children make mud-pies and play at soldiers, just as English children do. The girls have their dolls and the boys their tops and kites. The babies are very fat, rosy little things, and every one of them is encouraged from its earliest infancy to eat as much as it possibly can, and even more than it wants. An enormous appetite is regarded as a most desirable possession in Korea.

The Koreans are not very tall, but they are well made. Their faces are oval, and their skin dark in colour. Although the children are often very ruddy, their hair is dark, yet not so black as to please the Koreans, who admire very dark hair, and even use hair-dye to change it if it is too light to suit their taste. The faces one sees in the streets are generally like the Chinese, with high cheeks and narrow eyes, yet sometimes a Korean might almost be mistaken for a European; but this is more common among the upper than among the working classes. As a nation, the Koreans are apt to be idle, and careless of the morrow; and though they are not really brave, this carelessness and indifference lead them sometimes to take risks which the bravest Westerner would shrink from. Thus, in districts where

The Women and Children

tigers are numerous, the people constantly sleep with their house-doors open, and a curious instance of this indifference to obvious peril is afforded in the case of two Koreans who lay down to sleep with their heads actually pillowed on the rails of the electric tramway!

When roused, the Koreans are very passionate and they sometimes even take their own lives in a fit of anger. In the old days, quarrels between one family and another were numerous, and it was quite usual for a man to receive from his father a coat, which he was not to take off until he had avenged the family honour for some real or fancied insult. Whatever the Koreans may have been in days of yore (and it is on record that they were mighty men of valour), they are at the present day usually more anxious to avoid than to provoke conflict. But when hard pressed, they fight with desperate valour. When the forts of Kang-poa were attacked by the Americans in 1871, the hard-pressed defenders, even after being disarmed, continued to fight with stones and handfuls of dust, and many of them obstinately refused quarter.

Korean women, with the exception of some of the ladies of good family and the *gesang*,

Korea

or dancing-girls, who are chosen for their good looks, are distressingly plain. Hard work may account for much of this: for if the Korean man is idle, his wife is a model of patient industry. She labours all day in the house or in the fields, and often sits up half the night to wash and prepare the long white coats without which no self-respecting married man will be seen abroad. When the wife has a little leisure, she seeks the society of the other women, for home-life, as we understand it, is unknown in Korea. The average husband regards his home merely as a place in which he can eat and sleep. His day's work over, his evening meal consumed, he likes to change his working clothes for one of the spotless white coats which his wife has " got up " for him, and, long pipe in hand, to join the groups of men which gather nightly round the wells and in the market-places. Except in very rare cases, it does not occur to him that his wife can be of any practical use, except to take care of his house and his children and to cook and wash for him.

The Western idea of the wife—the " helpmeet " whose sympathy and advice can often sustain and guide her husband—is opposed to

The Women and Children

all usage and tradition in Korea, and, indeed, in the East generally. In the Hermit Kingdom a wife is chosen carefully by the parents for the dowry she will bring, or for her beauty, or for her qualities for a housewife; but to those qualities of mind and heart which go to make up our idea of a good wife and mother not a thought is given. And those same qualities which, one cannot doubt, are found in many a Korean woman have, indeed, little chance of developing amid the ceaseless toil which is her portion after marriage.

A woman is given no names of her own, and she is simply described as the daughter, the wife, or the mother of So-and-so—always one of the sterner sex! Although legally women have no existence, they yet enjoy some special privileges. For instance, they can ride in their chairs past the Palace-gates, where all men are compelled to descend and to go on foot; and, until some six years ago, a strange custom, now fallen into disuse, gave over the street of Seoul entirely to the women from sunset until 1 a.m. As the sun sank the Great Bell was sounded, and every man hastened indoors, for to disregard this signal was to incur severe penalties; and then came forth from their seclusion ladies of high degree, upon whom, since their childhood, no man save those of their own family had ever looked. Attended by maids with lanterns, they passed through the streets to visit their female friends and relations, and one can imagine how they revelled in the liberty denied them during daylight.

Koreans adore their children, and the Chinese custom of getting rid of girl-babies by exposure to the elements is unknown among them. Boys are, of course, the most greatly desired, and if a man has no son of his own he will adopt one, in order that the rites for his departed spirit "may be properly performed."

The population of the country increases but slowly, infant mortality being very great.

The number of the blind in Korea is remarkable, as is the confidence with which they move along the roads, and even in the crowded streets. I have more than once only become aware of the affliction of a passer-by through narrowly escaping violent contact with him, so little did his gait and bearing suggest one who was sightless. Entirely confined to the blind is the calling of *pausee*, or soothsayers, whose business it is to

A KOREAN BRIDEGROOM. *Page 3.*

The Women and Children

cast horoscopes, and to determine propitious times and places for the celebration of marriage or funeral ceremonies. The Koreans are naturally a noisy people, and to talk very loud in company is considered the height of good manners. Boys are made to learn their lessons by shouting them at the top of their voices, and it may be that the powerful vocal organs for which the men are remarkable are in part due to this early habit. As sportsmen they do not excel. The calling of a hunter is regarded as a low one, and is only followed as a means of livelihood. The huntsmen usually disguise themselves in feathers and leaves, and as they stalk their prey they seek to attract it or to disarm suspicion by imitating the cries of birds and animals. Some of the tiger-hunters are brave, and will even follow the tiger into his cave before attacking him. The skin of the Manchurian tiger, found in the North of Korea, is very valuable. The teeth, claws, and blood all fetch large prices as medicines, while men eat the heart to make them brave.

Like the Chinese, the Koreans consider age as being in itself most honourable. They think it very polite indeed to inquire the age of a guest. When I used to call on the ladies of Seoul, they

Korea

always asked first how old I was, and then if I were married.

Koreans have enormous appetites, and nothing comes amiss to them—meal, fish (raw or cooked), vegetables, grains, and fruit. Some of them eat dogs, but this is not considered a very nice thing to do. Strange to say, although Korea lies between the two tea-drinking countries *par excellence*, " the cup that cheers " is almost unknown there. Meals are served on low tables, the family and guests squatting on the floor, and wooden spoons and chopsticks are used. The official language of the country is Chinese, which is taught in all schools, while public examinations are held in that tongue. The Korean language can be written in a syllabary, the characters of which are said to have been introduced into the country by Buddhist priests in the fourth century *anno Domini*. I tried to learn this syllabary, and shall not soon forget the way in which my native teacher and I used to shout it at the top of our voices. One of the lines (which you read downwards) was like a series of sneezes !

CHAPTER II

KOREAN SUPERSTITIONS

THE Koreans are not a brave people. I suppose it is impossible they should be so, seeing that for years the policy of the "Hermit Nation," as Korea has been called, has been to shut herself up from the outside world. And so, like men who have never pitted their strength against their fellows, the Koreans have no confidence in themselves. They are a simple, kindly people, easily pleased, easily astonished. They are very superstitious, and their lives from the cradle to the grave are hedged in by strange ceremonies. They believe that the air, the water, the mountains, and the forests are abodes of spirits, who are harmful to human beings if not constantly kept in good humour. There are, say the Koreans, benevolent spirits too, but they are not nearly so numerous or so powerful as the wicked ones.

When anyone falls ill, and when the cattle die, or when the rice-crop fails, the *mutang*, or witch,

Korea

must be consulted. She is supposed to be "possessed" by the spirits, and therefore able to understand and interpret their wishes, and to explain why they are angry. She also suggests what will please them most and induce them to remove the misfortunes they have caused. If it is a case of illness, the *mutang* will say that some offended spirit has taken up its abode in the house, and must be exorcised. This is done by means of a dance, accompanied by music and doleful songs.

Once I saw a witch-dance. I was passing along one of the streets of Seoul, when I heard sounds of music coming from one of the houses. As the door was open, I peeped in, and this is what I beheld: An excited-looking woman, in a long blue robe and a hat with a scarlet plume, was dancing and at the same time twisting a huge knife in each hand. Several girls sat round, beating drums and singing a monotonous chant, their eyes fixed on the dancing *mutang*. Faster and faster she sprang from one foot to another, and ever faster whirled the knives, until at last she sank in an exhausted heap on the floor. We were told that the master of the house was very sick indeed. Truly it must be a terrible thing to be ill in a country where even quietness

Korean Superstitions

is denied to the sufferer. And yet I am not sure that the witch-dance, with all its accompanying horrors of drums and flutes, is not to be preferred to the native doctor, who comes armed with pincers and hot irons, his pockets filled with such nauseous remedies as dried tiger's blood and bones.

Now as to the forms and ceremonies which are connected with weddings. In the first place, no two people with the same clan or surname are allowed to marry. Again, the horoscopes of the proposed bride and bridegroom must be drawn up and carefully compared by one of the astrologers, and the omens consulted, in order to see if everything is favourable to the marriage. Let us imagine a case in which everything has turned out quite satisfactorily. On the morning of the great day the bridegroom's boy-friends assemble at his home to assist in the ceremony of " downing the tuft," as the Korean phrase goes. His hair, which he has worn hitherto in a long pigtail, must be combed up and fixed on the crown of his head in a tight knot. This is the mark of the married man, and in Korea the unmarried man is not regarded as a man at all, but only as a child. Of the three ways of addressing

Korea

people, the third and most familiar, used towards children and inferiors, is always employed by everyone in speaking to him. In the councils and assemblies of the men he can take no part, and everywhere he finds himself obliged to give way to chubby boy-bridegrooms of twelve or fourteen. One solitary privilege the despised bachelor enjoys over his married contemporaries. Should he offend against the law, he receives the lenient treatment which would be given to a child!

Let us now return to our bride and bridegroom. Whilst the boy, with the help of his late playfellows, is turning himself into a man, the girl, in her home, is doing her best to look like a woman. Her hair is loosely twisted up and secured with silver pins, and, arrayed in all her best clothes and thickly veiled, she is carried in a closed chair to her future home. Her relations and friends walk with her in a procession, at the head of which is carried a goose, the emblem of faithfulness. The wedding ceremony consists of a certain number of bows, which show mutual consent. Then the bride's veil is taken off, and the newly-made husband sees his wife for perhaps the first time. For the first three or four days of her

Korean Superstitions

married life the girl is expected not to utter a single word, and I am sorry to say that all her friends make a point of going to see her, in order to tease her and get her to speak!

Then, there are the forms to be observed at the moment of death. As the last breath is drawn one of near kin to the dying person must call upon the good spirits, asking them to receive the departing soul. Otherwise it will not be received into the invisible community, and must wander solitary for ever.

The rules which regulate mourning for the dead are very strict. A son mourns for his father three years, and during that time he wears robes of grass-cloth with a huge hat that almost conceals his face, the rest of which he is supposed to cover with his fan. In old days a mourner was not obliged to answer anyone who spoke to him. Hence, to the first missionaries who came to Korea, and at the peril of their lives travelled through the country, the mourner's dress offered a singularly safe disguise.

Among other curious superstitions the people of Seoul believe that underneath the city sleeps a great dragon, its patron and guardian. While I was in the country there was a great drought,

Korea

and the people decided among themselves that the dragon was annoyed because the tram-lines recently laid down were pressing upon his tail, and so disturbing his sleep. So they rose up one night and destroyed the lines, breaking up as many of the trams as they could get hold of.

CHAPTER III

ABOUT GINSENG AND OTHER THINGS

A WONDERFUL plant is grown in Korea which is called ginseng. It is bought chiefly by the Chinese, who believe that tea made from its roots will give people health and strength, and make them live to a very great age. There is a place in Korea called Song-do, where all the fields are planted with ginseng, and in each field there are little platforms on four posts. On these boys sit all night, watching to see that thieves do not come to steal the precious plants. All night long you may hear them shouting, to keep away the robbers, and partly, I suspect, to keep up their own courage. In October the ginseng is pulled up, boiled, dried in the sun, and then the greater part of it is packed up in boxes to go to China. No one really knows why the Chinese think ginseng such a wonderful medicine. All that is known is that it has been used for a very long time indeed, and that now it is actually worth more than its weight in gold.

Korea

When I was at Song-do a Korean nobleman came there who had been so unfortunate as to offend the Emperor, and he asked the friends with whom I was staying if he might hide in their house. He really seemed to consider himself in a good deal of danger, and never joined us in the veranda until nightfall, keeping entirely to his own room during the day. In Korea, if one were unfortunate enough to offend the Emperor, it was often wise to disappear for a time, until one's friends should bring news that it was safe to come out. It used to make me think of the poor gardeners whom Alice saw in the White Queen's Garden in Wonderland. You remember the Queen was very angry indeed because the roses were white instead of red; and the gardeners were extremely frightened when they saw how angry she was and heard her say, " Off with their heads!" So they fell on their faces; and as they were really playing-cards and were quite flat, the Queen walked on without seeing them, and very soon forgot how angry she had been with them. And in somewhat the same way in Korea it was a wise thing to disappear entirely for a time if you had offended the Emperor, and probably he would quite forget how angry he had been with

About Ginseng and Other Things

you. I am glad to say it was so with our nobleman. He lived in the house for a week, and at the end of that time his friends told him that it was quite safe for him to be seen about again.

The Korean nobleman, or *yangban*, is a very grand person indeed. When he goes out, his chair is carried by eight bearers, who advance at a quick trot, while at the same time they shout loudly, so that all may know that a great man is coming. In summer the ordinary wooden sides of the chair, which is just like a box slung on poles, are taken out, and sides of black horsehair netting are put in, so that the whole thing really looks like a large meat-safe. Sometimes the *yangban* goes out on horse- or donkey-back, perched on an enormous saddle, in front of which is fixed a handle. The *yangban* holds firmly on to this, while his *mapoo*, or groom, leads his animal by the bridle, and two other servants run beside him, holding his feet in the stirrups. You see, it is considered extremely aristocratic and fashionable to be very helpless, so if our *yangban* should be obliged to walk a few steps, he must be supported by his attendants on either side. The everyday costume of these gentry consists of a gauze dress of a beautiful dark blue over a

Korea

silk robe. With this is worn a small tight-fitting cap of fine black horsehair, on each side of which are fixed two small carved pieces, said to represent the ever-attentive ears of the courtier. On the front of his robe the *yangban* wears an embroidered design representing a tiger, a dragon, or a phœnix. These show the degree of official rank possessed by the wearer. When I was in the country numbers of these badges of office were always to be had for sale—a fact well accounted for by the very constant changes which then took place among the official classes of Korea. All appointments were dependent on the pleasure of the Emperor, who in a fit of anger would sometimes condemn one of his Ministers to one or two years' banishment in some remote district of his domain. As the Imperial wrath was happily short-lived, you were quite likely to meet the exiled official a week or two later on his way to the Palace, and to hear of his having received a higher appointment than he had enjoyed previous to his disgrace. It was all rather like a comic opera.

CHAPTER IV

A VISIT TO THE EMPEROR

I REALLY felt quite excited as I dressed myself in my best to attend an audience given by the Emperor of Korea. There is always something very interesting about a palace, especially the palace of an Eastern ruler, which you imagine must be like the beautiful ones described in fairy-tales. People tell you that if you expect a thing to be very wonderful indeed, you will generally be disappointed, and I think that it does turn out so very often. I certainly was disappointed when I walked through the big palace gates into a very untidy courtyard. A guide was waiting there to conduct us to the Emperor, and in order to follow him we had to jump over several large pools of water.

We at length reached the door of the palace, and were conducted along a corridor and ushered into a room at the end of it. Now, I thought, I shall see something gorgeous and wonderful. But

Korea

what I did see might have been a farmhouse parlour in England. There was a Brussels carpet with a pattern of large pink roses, a square table in the middle of the room, surrounded by mahogany chairs stuffed with horsehair. We sat on these uncomfortable chairs and drank cups of tea until we were summoned to the Emperor's presence. Now, I had hoped the Emperor would have been sitting on a throne, dressed in beautiful robes, and surrounded by his greatest men. On the contrary, he stood in the corner of a small room furnished in the Korean fashion, which means scarcely furnished at all, and with an ordinary deal table in front of him. The Crown Prince and the baby Prince, aged about four, stood beside him. We all of us advanced in turn, shook hands with him, and at the same time made the best curtsy we could manage.

After this ceremony, there followed a short conversation with the Emperor, through the interpreters, in the course of which he hoped we were all well, and made other civil enquiries. We then learnt that an entertainment had been provided for us, and that we were invited or commanded (for is not a royal invitation a command?) to dine in the palace. The entertain-

A Visit to the Emperor

ment, which was an exhibition of dancing by the *gesang*, or professional dancers, was very pretty indeed. The orchestra sat on the floor, dressed in scarlet robes, and played on curious stringed instruments. The first dance—a slow and graceful one—was performed by girls wearing blue dresses and with flowers in their hair. Then a model of a boat was dragged in, and while the orchestra played a wild air, suggesting stormy winds and raging seas, some of the dancers got into the boat, which was violently rocked about, while others danced round, impersonating the spirits of the storm. The prettiest dance of all, I thought, was danced by one girl all by herself. She was dressed in a long yellow robe, and her sleeves hung down far below her hands. This was called the Dance of the Golden Oriole, a beautiful bird which is often seen in Korea. Very prettily this girl imitated the movements of a bird, raising her arm so that her long sleeves hung down like wings.

After the dances were over we had dinner, which, rather to our disappointment, was just like an English one, and so I shall not describe it.

CHAPTER V

THE HISTORY OF THE PEOPLE

KOREANS tell you that the history of their country goes back for 3,000 years. They owe to China their laws, their culture, and civilization—all of which, they say, came to them in 1122 B.C. In that year Thi Tize was, for some reason, exiled from the Celestial Kingdom, and, with a large band of Chinese, he made his way over to Korea, or, as it was then called, Chosen, or " Land of the Morning Calm." When the Chinese arrived they found the natives living in caves and burrows, clothing themselves in skins, and eating roots and the flesh of such animals as they could bring down with their flint arrows. These natives died out or inter-married with the new-comers, who brought with them the arts and learning of China, and their knowledge passed, through Korea, on to the island kingdom of Japan.

Until 107 B.C.—so we are told—Chosen remained an independent kingdom, but in that

MR. KIM KUI HAI, LATE INTERPRETER
TO THE BRITISH LEGATION

The History of the People

year she was conquered by China, and became subject to her. Afterwards, there arose a new set of Kings, of the tribe of the Koraians, who gave their name to the kingdom, and for 600 years held it against the Chinese, whom they had driven out. At the end of that time the country was again conquered by China.

We now come to real history. In 912, Kung-wo, a Buddhist monk, raised the standard of rebellion against China, and with success. He was proclaimed King, but was soon afterwards assassinated by his lieutenant, Wang, one of the old ruling house of the Koraians, who some years later on became the first real King of Korea. The later rulers of his dynasty, which lasted several centuries, seem to have misused their power, and Korea groaned under terrible oppressions. At length a deliverer of the people arose, in the person of Ni Taijo, a man of lowly origin but of good abilities. He was raised to the throne by the people of Korea, whose choice he fully justified during the course of a long reign. He it was who established Confucianism in the State, and under him examinations in the Chinese classics were instituted and the dress and customs of China were formally adopted. Yang, the modern Seoul,

Korea

became the capital, and has remained so ever since.

In the year 1592, during the reign of the Emperor Hideyoshi, the Japanese made a determined effort to obtain possession of Korea. In the month of May a large army landed at Fusan and marched to Seoul, leaving behind it a line of ruined and deserted villages. The capital was found to contain only the aged and infirm, who had not been able to join the hurried flight of the Court to Ping Yang. Thither the Japanese followed; there they met and utterly defeated the Korean army, capturing the city of Ping Yang. A panic overtook the unfortunate Koreans at the sight of these invaders, armed, not with the familiar bow and arrows, but with matchlocks, never before seen by them. At the approach of the rigorous winter of Northern China the Japanese decided to remain at Ping Yang until the spring, and orders were despatched to their fleet, then lying at Fusan, to move round the coast to the mouth of the river. At this point the invaders received an unexpected check, for their fleet was attacked and almost entirely destroyed by the now desperate Koreans. Their source of supplies thus cut off, the Japanese were

The History of the People

rendered still more uneasy by news of the approach of a Chinese army sent to assist the Koreans. On New Year's Day, 1593, the allied armies of China and Korea appeared before Ping Yang, and the Japanese, seeing themselves outnumbered, retreated to Seoul, where they fortified themselves.

Famine had, however, appeared in the land of Korea. Both armies suffered greatly, and all longed for peace; a treaty was therefore drawn up, according to the terms of which the invaders evacuated Seoul and returned to the southern coast, where they established fortified camps.

A second Japanese invasion occurred in 1597, and was again opposed by a Chinese army. The first fortress taken by the Japanese was that of Nan-on. According to the barbarous customs of the age, the ears of all the slain defenders were cut off and sent to Kioto, where the " Mound of Ears " is still shown. This invasion failed, like the other, through the destruction of the Japanese navy. Hideyoshi died in 1598, leaving orders for the recall of all his troops. Until 1878 the Japanese retained possession of the port of Fusan, and here trade was briskly carried on between the two nations. The Koreans exchanged earthen

Korea

pots, dried fish, ginseng, and walnuts for Ja
swords and other military equipments.
year some important men went from Seo
gifts for the Great Lord, who was call
Tycoon, at Tokyo. In the year 1637 a
people called the Manchus, who were con
China, thought they would like to conquer
as well. They captured the King, who p
to help them in attacking Peking, which
capital of China.

As a reward for this, the Manchus allow
Koreans to keep the Chinese style of c
and hair-dressing, which they always used
the poor Chinese, who had made a brave s
for freedom, were compelled to shave thei
and wear pigtails like the Manchus; and
why Chinamen wear pigtails to the prese
From the time that the Manchus began
in China, Korea was numbered among the
belonging to China, and she had to send a
of money every year to the Capital City,
This went on up to our own times, when
urged by Japan, rose in rebellion, and n
to throw off the yoke of China, becomin
time a free country once more.

CHAPTER VI

A JOURNEY TO PING YANG

THIS is an account of a voyage we made to Ping Yang, which we were anxious to see, as it is one of the oldest walled cities of Korea, and is also interesting as having been the scene of a battle during the Chino-Japanese War. We were staying at Chemulpo, the port of Seoul, and late one evening we heard that a Japanese steamer bound for Ping Yang was in the harbour. We took a boat and hurried on board at once, only to be told that that ship had no room for passengers, and that on this occasion she had already on board four American miners bound for the gold-mines, who were occupying the saloon. But the Japanese captain was unwilling to disappoint two ladies, and, as the hot weather was rapidly approaching, we did not want to postpone our journey; so at length it was decided that one of the officers should give up his cabin to us. We gratefully squeezed ourselves and our belongings

Korea

into the tiny apartment kindly placed at our disposal, and awoke the next morning to find ourselves just entering the mouth of the muddy river of Ping Yang, the waters of which are exactly the colour of a London fog. On either side were fields of rice and maize, backed by low green hills. We had comfortably established ourselves on camp-stools on deck, and were enjoying the sunshine, when a very astonished face suddenly appeared at the top of the companion ladder. We rightly guessed that this astonished and rugged face, crowned with a mane of carroty hair, belonged to one of our fellow-travellers, the miners, who had all been asleep when we came on board the evening before. The others soon followed, and after they had got over their astonishment at finding two English ladies, when they had only expected to see Japanese and Koreans, we became quite friendly. They told us they had come from America, practically penniless, and with only the clothes they stood up in (and those were more patches than anything else). We met these men a year afterwards in Japan, looking extremely prosperous and well dressed as the result of their gold-digging!

At Chinampo, where we stopped for a few

A Journey to Ping Yang

hours, we were entertained by the Commissioner of Customs, who represented in his single person the English, French, and American Consuls. Here the number of our European passengers was increased by the arrival of a French missionary Father, who wore a long black robe called a soutane, which contrasted with his white sun-helmet. He belonged to the Société des Missions Étrangers, and told us that the missionaries of this society in Korea numbered about forty, and their converts between 30,000 and 40,000. He was then on his way to administer extreme unction to a dying member of his flock, and to reach him would travel sixty miles by boat and still further on foot after leaving the steamer.

The next day we arrived at Ping Yang, where we stayed with some American missionaries in their pleasant house just outside the city. On the other side of it lies the plain of Ping Yang, the scene of the great battle. It is curious to think that in this fight the opposing armies were those of two nations closely allied in race and language, and yet one of them was provided with all the latest inventions of modern warfare, while the other could only show the weapons and methods of almost medieval times.

Korea

An eyewitness who saw the Chinese embark at Taku described them as a sort of ragged regiment, armed with ancient matchlocks, spears, and tridents. The greater number of these poor fellows were really " pressed " men, agriculturists and coolies, who knew little or nothing about fighting. Many of them carried their umbrellas and fans, and even cages containing birds, to which the Chinese are devoted. An undisciplined force such as this could not hold its own before the guns and rifles and the perfect discipline of the Japanese. After a terrible fight on the plain the Chinese made a desperate attempt to hold the old fort which overlooks it; but the Japanese, each one arming himself with the branch of a fir-tree, so that on their swift and silent way up the slope they might seem to be a part of the woods which cover it, stole up and utterly routed them.

Ping Yang city is built in the shape of a boat, and is, the people will tell you, attached to a post, which they show you on the plain. They really think that if anyone were to pull up this post, the city would be in danger of floating away down the river. Ping Yang is famed for the beauty of its women, but as they all wear dome-shaped hats

A Journey to Ping Yang

4 yards in circumference, one has no chance of seeing what their faces are like.

When we left Ping Yang, we had to make the journey down the river in a fishing-boat, or junk, as there was no steamer to suit us.

We decided to start at four o'clock one afternoon, and at that hour we repaired to the appointed place of embarkation. Most of the Korean rivers are bordered with stretches of more or less solid mud, into which, according to the consistency, one sinks ankle or knee deep. These mud-flats are the homes of numbers of mud-coloured crabs; they are not at all timid, and, indeed, seem to take a pleasure in watching one's struggles in the slime, over which they scamper sideways on slender pink legs. At length we gained the water's edge, and by means of a plank reached the deck of our vessel, into which was hoisted our scanty luggage and provisions for two days, including fresh water, for that of the river is not fit to drink.

The boatmen, four in number, received us with the really graceful bows which seem to come natural to the Koreans; then, with many professions of esteem, and with smiles and compliments, they showed us the awful-looking " cabin "

Korea

prepared for us. The only way of entering it was to jump from the deck, and no sooner had you done this than you longed to get out again, so very stuffy and grimy was it. Its dimensions were 4 feet by 4 feet, and it was lined with yellow oil-paper. When darkness fell we descended into this unattractive shelter, and there we passed a terrible night, which has left behind it a confused impression of cramped limbs, biting insects, and mournful Korean songs, which one or another of our men seemed to keep up unceasingly. Dawn found us on deck, with a strong breeze behind us. We slipped quickly down the river, reaching Chinampo, where we were to join the steamer, about seven o'clock that evening. Here we paid our boatmen with long strings of copper cash. These are pierced and strung on coarse twine, and about 1,000 go to a yen (value 2s.).

CHAPTER VII

THE CLOTHES OF THE KOREANS

SOME very pretty things are made in Korea. For instance, there are the fans which are carried in summer-time by every man, woman, and child. They are made of coloured paper which has been soaked in oil, and when they are held up against the sun, they look like pieces of stained glass.

Then, the women do beautiful embroideries for dresses, hangings, and for the badges of rank, which every great man wears on the front of his robe. I have seen most wonderful embroidered screens in Korea: one, in particular, I remember, which would be a joy in an English nursery. It was covered with battle-scenes, in which blue and pink and mauve horses carried green-bearded warriors, who fought with bows and arrows and strange weapons like tridents.

One of the palaces contains some marvellous wall-paintings, which always used to remind me

Korea

of the "jabberwock" and the other queer animals which Alice heard about in her journey through "Looking-glass Land."

The shops in Seoul are full of silks and gauzes in the prettiest colours, of ribbons, of strings of coral and amber, which are used as hat-strings; of cabinets and boxes, in black lacquer, ornamented with mother-of-pearl, or covered with lacquer in brilliant green and red. You may wander round a shop at your will, and handle all these pretty things, and the owner, who is almost certain to be smoking a pipe with a stem about a yard long, will sit quietly in the corner and watch you dreamily. If you decide to buy something and ask him the price, he probably regards you with a sort of mild reproach as a disturber of his peace. The Koreans never seem to care to make money unless they are really in want of it, when they become very eager indeed. As we walk down the street in search of pretty things to buy, we may very likely chance to see a *yangban* from some distant part of the country reclining in his mule-litter, the poles of which are fastened to the backs of two mules. We are certain to see many closed chairs, containing ladies, whose chubby little girl-attendants run breathlessly alongside,

The Clothes of the Koreans

keeping up with the steady jog-trot of the chair-coolies. We shall probably be jostled by groups of blind men walking arm-in-arm, three or four in a row. Blindness is very common as a result of smallpox, which is one of the great scourges of the country. So many children die from it that a Korean mother, if asked the number of her children, will only tell you of those who have had the smallpox and recovered from it.

If you should happen to be, after nightfall, in a quiet place near the city of Seoul, you will hear coming from every direction a low, regular tapping sound. This means that the Korean women are hard at work " getting-up " the long white coats in which their husbands make such a brave show. These coats have been previously washed in some of the many streams which run through the city. Were you to peep into one of the houses from which the tapping comes, you would find a woman squatting on the ground before a large board; on this the coat is spread, and she is beating it with two pieces of wood, like small rolling-pins, one of which she holds in either hand. This is her curious way of ironing. A strange thing about Korean clothes is that they are not sewn, but are gummed together, and so they have

Korea

to be taken to pieces every time they are washed, and put together again afterwards!

Korean men wear baggy trousers, tied at the ankle, one or two short coats, and sometimes three or four long coats over these. The clothes of poor people are made of cotton, and those of the rich of silk or transparent gauze. As to hats, I really do not know how many different shapes there are; but it is a fact that by looking at a man's hat you can usually learn something of his position and circumstances. For instance, there is the married man's hat, that of the bridegroom, the mourner, the scholar, the priest, the chairman, the messenger, the coolie, and many more. They are all made either of split bamboo or of horsehair.

The women, except in certain districts, wear no hats, but in Seoul they cover their heads with a green silk coat, of which the sleeves hang loosely down. They tell you that this custom dates from a day, many hundreds of years ago, when an enemy attacked the city while all the men were away hunting. Luckily, they had left their coats behind them, and the women had just time to throw these over their heads and to rush on to the walls. When the enemy saw the coats,

The Clothes of the Koreans

they thought the men must have come back, and fled in terror. Ever since then the women of Seoul have had the right to wear their coats in the funny way described above.

Korean women wear very full skirts, usually white or pale blue, and short bodices, white, red, or green, tied with ribbons at the left side. During the winter season, which is very severe, both men and women wear padded clothes, and, if they can afford it, as many as six or seven, so that they seem to get fatter and fatter as the cold increases. Poor folks who cannot afford this generally walk about for four months in the year with their arms folded inside their loose coats.

CHAPTER VIII

THE PEOPLE AND THEIR BELIEFS

KOREANS are Buddhists by religion. Many temples are to be found in the country, chiefly on the tops of hills and mountains. In these temples there is always an altar of red lacquer, and on it figures of Buddha and his disciples, several bronze or lacquered candlesticks, and vases filled with flowers. On a table in front of it you will usually see plates containing offerings of cakes and fruit. Generally you will find a priest singing in a droning voice, and perhaps another priest may be beating the sacred drum. These drums are often things of beauty, ornamented with paintings and fine carving. I took a great fancy to one which was in a temple near Seoul, and much wanted the priests to let me have it, in exchange for a new one, but after some consideration my offer was rejected.

The priests and monks who lived in the monastery belonging to this temple were always very

KOREAN GIRL IN WINTER DRESS. Page 39.

The People and their Beliefs

pleased to see us. They would invite us into their refectory, and regale us with persimmons and chestnuts. All these monks wore rather dirty yellow robes, and their heads were shaven as smooth as billiard-balls. The monasteries are chiefly supported by the younger monks, who go round the country with their begging-bowls, and even the very poorest will not refuse to give them at least a handful of rice.

Koreans, like the Chinese, worship their ancestors. In every house, no matter how humble, there is a shelf on which are oblong black tablets, inscribed in gold letters with the names of dead members of the family. Rich people devote a room or a separate building to the keeping of these precious memorials, which are supposed also to provide a resting-place for the spirits, should they wish to revisit their old home. Happily, it is not only the dead ancestors who are venerated, but the living ones also. Parents and grandparents are treated with immense respect. Even men and women long past middle age will defer, as a matter of course, to the wishes of the old people. Like the Chinese, Koreans consider " filial duty " as one of the greatest virtues, and some of the most charming fairy-tales of both nations deal

Korea

with the reward of the dutiful, and, *per contra*, the punishment of the disobedient child. The twenty-four instances of filial piety, as limned by a Chinese artist, have a great vogue in Korea. One of the nicest is the story of the son who fancied that his parents felt sad because they were growing old. So he dressed himself like a child, and gambolled about the garden with some toys, for he said to himself: " If they see me playing about as if I were only five years old instead of fifty, they may fancy, if only for a moment, that they are young again, and that may give them pleasure!"

There was another son who, on a hot summer's afternoon, covered himself with honey, and lay down beside his parents, who were about to take their afternoon nap. He did this so that the flies, which are very troublesome in China, should come to him instead of worrying his father and mother!

CHAPTER IX

A KOREAN HOUSE

I WANT you to make believe that you are coming to see me in my Korean house. Let us imagine that you have arrived in a chair which, made of wicker and slung on poles, is carried by four men. You have been dumped down before the heavy wooden gates, your chairmen lustily calling for the *moonjiggie,* or porter. You must not be surprised if you should have to wait some time, for the *moonjiggie* is a leisurely creature, and if, at the time of your arrival, he should happen to have been engaged in the all-important business of eating, he will very likely finish his meal before attending to your summons. When he does at length put his head out of his little window, you must, in answer to his look of mild inquiry, pronounce these words : *Pouen isso* (literally " Lady is "). As you are coming to see me by invitation, his answer will, of course, be *Isso* (is), not *Upso* (is not). Thereupon you must hand

Korea

him your card, and, having received it, he
fling open the big wooden gates, and invite
to enter and to follow him up the ga:
path. My *amah* (maid) will receive the
and will conduct you to the drawing-room
windows of which open on to the veranda.
first thing to strike you on entering will
ably be the ceiling, whose rafters are like th
an English sixteenth-century house, dark
heavy, the interstices filled with yellow
paper.

A Korean house is built in the foll
way : First, four corner posts are planted
in the ground ; then the beams which
port the roof and those which divide the
into rooms are placed between them. All
posts are notched at the top, and into
notches the cross-beams are fitted. The f
work of the house being completed, the next
is to put the roof on. Last of all, the wa
added, of wattle, covered with plaster, lined
with oil-paper.

While we are sitting in the drawing-
you may perhaps hear a cat mew be
your feet. This will be the voice of my
haired kitten, and I must explain to yo

A Korean House

it is that he is able to walk about under the floor in this surprising way. All Korean houses are built on a hollow foundation, through which run narrow passages, formed by flat stones set upright in rows. At one end of the house is built a small furnace, in which wood and dried leaves are burned; the heat from this goes into the passages or flues, and the smoke finds its way out by a chimney running up the opposite wall. This method of warming houses is common all over China and Korea. But, like most Europeans in these countries, I prefer to use a coal-stove, and so the disused *kang*—as this arrangement of flues is called—has become a hunting-ground for our own and other people's cats. The worst of it is that, once in, they find it very hard to get out again.

Soon there probably appears on the veranda a queer bunchy white figure, who, smiling all over her work-worn face, makes you three or four profound bows. This is Pak, my second *amah*, washerwoman and mender to the household. She is a trustworthy and laborious creature. Could Pak be set down to one of those old-fashioned confession-books, to which one was supposed to confide one's most secret thoughts,

Korea

her answer to the questions, "Your favourite occupation," "Your favourite amusement," and "Your favourite game," would assuredly be "Work."

She is a monomaniac on the subject, and when, as happens occasionally, there is nothing to wash and nothing to mend, the shapeless form of poor old Pak, in her voluminous petticoats, wanders round uneasily, peering in anxiously at doors and windows. Sometimes the sight so moves me that I positively feel inclined to make work for her by tearing off buttons and strings. When I have found her something to do, Pak, with a loud clap of her hands and a look of real gratitude, rushes forward to receive it, and is perfectly happy until again she has a moment of leisure. On this special occasion we are imagining Pak has no doubt only appeared in order that she may exchange salutations with you, and this ceremony concluded, she will depart quite satisfied. During your visit to me you are almost certain to see my Chinese cook, for it is his custom to wait until I have a caller, and then to enter and announce a scarcity in the commissariat. Introducing himself into the room with a sidelong motion, he stands smiling with mingled slyness and depreca-

A Korean House

tion. "Bl—d no," "Su—g no," he announces, by which I am to understand that the supplies of bread and sugar have run out. If he can do this just before a meal, his delight is unbounded, and he chuckles to himself as I send the garden coolie rushing off to Ai Tai, the Chinese storekeeper.

When Wong first entered our service, he evidently imagined it to be an ideal field for the exercise of "squeeze-pigeon." The first week's bill submitted to us, with the various items written out in single columns, reached the astonishing length (for we measured it) of $29\frac{1}{2}$ inches. According to this document, we two, with one dog and a cat—for the servants all go home for their meals—had consumed in the course of seven days 24 pounds of beef, ninety-seven eggs, and other things in proportion!

CHAPTER X

A KOREAN FAIRY-TALE

ONCE the King of the fishes was very ill indeed, and his Court physicians could do nothing for him, although they tried their very hardest to cure him, and although they consulted all the medical books which are written on the pebbles at the bottom of the river. At length the turtle, whom no one thought of consulting, came forward, and announced that he had been told in a dream that the King could be cured by a poultice made of a rabbit's eye; and, being most anxious to please the King and to distinguish himself, he offered to get the eye himself. He hoped to be able to manage this, as he had a bowing acquaintance with a rabbit which often came along the river-bank. One morning Master Rabbit appeared, looking very smart, the sun shining on his brown coat, and his ear cocked at just the fashionable angle. "Good-morning," said the turtle; and "Good-morning," returned the rabbit. "How

MONUMENT WITH TORTOISE PEDESTAL
IN THE PUBLIC GARDENS, SEOUL

A Korean Fairy-Tale

beautiful the world looks to-day!" "Yes," said the turtle; "but your dry upper world is not a patch on our world, the water, where our King, in a golden palace, sits on a pearl throne, guarded by fishes in shining armour, and where the trees and flowers are of all the colours of the rainbow." "Really, I should like to see all this," said Master Rabbit; "but, of course, that is impossible." "Not in the least," answered the turtle, "if you will trust yourself to me. Get on my back, and I will take you down to see His Majesty." After a few moments' hesitation, the rabbit agreed, and, holding on to the turtle as well as he could, he soon found himself at the bottom of the river and in the presence of the ailing monarch. Sitting on a gold stool, and while eating the most delightful river sweetmeats, Mr. Bunny overheard someone say, "Now is the time to take the rabbit's eye," and he began to feel very uncomfortable indeed. Fortunately, he was a clever rabbit and had all his wits about him, and he managed not to show that he was really very much frightened. He turned very politely to the turtle, who was standing beside him: "Do I understand that one of my eyes is required for the King's service?" On hearing that it was, Mr. Rabbit said: "I

Korea

must explain to you that I have really two pairs of eyes—a real pair and a crystal pair, the latter of which I use for travelling, and that is the pair I am wearing at the present moment. If you will permit me to return home, I will fetch one of my real eyes, and shall have much pleasure in presenting it to His Majesty." All the fishes were glad to hear that they would get the rabbit's eye so easily, and without the trouble of killing him, and they gladly allowed the turtle to help him on shore again. And, as you will not be surprised to hear, immediately the rabbit found himself in his own familiar world again, he bounded away over the fields, and took care never to go near the river any more.

CHAPTER XI

HOW EUROPEANS FIRST WENT TO KOREA

IT is little more than thirty years since foreigners were able to enter the Hermit Kingdom, except in disguise. It is difficult to realize this now, as there are few countries where one is made so generally welcome. Everyone, almost without exception, meets you with smiles and kindly, if somewhat annoying, curiosity. Europeans are still to the country-people objects of wonder, and their dress and their habits are an inexhaustible source of amusement and surprise. I well remember my room in an up-country missionary's house being suddenly invaded by a laughing company of Korean women. I was in the act of pinning on my hat, and their astonishment at seeing the pins going, as they imagined, right through my head was very amusing to see. They proceeded to try the pins on their own heads, and were still more astonished at my curious ways.

Korea

The first foreigners who are known to have entered Korea were the few survivors of the Dutch ship *Hollandra*, which was wrecked on the west coast in the year 1627. One of these sailors, Jan Wetteree, spent the remainder of his life in Seoul, and seems to have occupied much the same position there as did the celebrated Bill Adams at the Court of Japan. In 1653 another Dutch vessel, the *Sparloche*, broke up on the rocky shores of the island of Quelpart, and thirty of her crew managed to swim to the mainland. They settled down amongst the Koreans, and several of them became officers of the King's household. One of them, named Hamel, escaped after fourteen years, and returned to his own country, where he wrote an account of his strange adventures. After this, for two hundred years the only Europeans who found their way into the country were the French missionaries, and to obtain entrance they were obliged to assume various disguises, and afterwards to live in hiding.

It is not now known why Korea should have adopted this policy of exclusion of all foreigners, which has caused her to be known as the " Hermit Kingdom," but it is certain that it has at most periods been rigidly enforced, and more particu-

How Europeans first went to Korea

larly since the middle of the seventeenth century. The Tai-ouen-koun, father of the late Emperor, was a stanch supporter of this policy. He was appointed Regent of Korea by the then Empress-Dowager, who, not having any children of her own, had adopted his son, Li-Hsi, then a mere child, and had made him heir to the throne. Six years previously, in 1860, the Allies had arrived before Peking, and had burned the Summer Palace. This had been followed by the establishment of Embassies in the Chinese capital, and by the opening to foreign commerce of several Chinese ports. Obviously, what had happened in China might occur in Korea also, and it was more the fear of this than any dislike to the Christian religion which prompted his relentless persecution of the Christians in 1866, in which six French priests lost their lives.

After the terrible massacre of that year, news of which was carried to Shanghai by one of the surviving priests, a French squadron was despatched to Korea. It anchored at the mouth of the River Han, and two gunboats were sent up to Seoul. This was the very first occasion on which the Koreans had seen vessels moving by steam, and the strange sight seemed to them full of terror. But the Tai-ouen-koun, " the man of the heart of stone," would offer no explanation or apology. The French Admiral, therefore, proceeded to land a party of Marines on the island of Kanghoa, which is situated on the river, halfway between Chemulpo and Seoul. There was on the island a monastery, which the Koreans had fortified. It stood at the end of a narrow pass, and as the Frenchmen marched carelessly up the narrow pass which led to it they were suddenly assailed from above with showers of stones and arrows. Unprepared as they were, there was nothing to be done but to beat a hasty retreat, and on the day following, for some inexplicable reason, and without making any attempt to retrieve their defeat, they sailed back to Shanghai.

This abandonment of the situation, of course, left the Koreans even more fatuously self-satisfied than they had been, and more than ever convinced of their superiority to all Western nations. In 1870 an attempt was made by the United States to open commercial relations with Korea, and a small squadron was despatched with this object. As the ships were passing Kanghoa, on their way to Seoul, they were fired on. The Americans

How Europeans first went to Korea

immediately landed upon the island, and, after destroying the forts, they abandoned their enterprise and sailed away.

The first commercial treaty signed by Korea was with Japan. This was in 1878, and it was followed shortly after by treaties with England, France, and Germany. There are now numerous treaty-ports, where foreign ships call almost daily.

CHAPTER XII

THE SIGHTS OF SEOUL

THE Emperor has three palaces in Seoul, called respectively the Northern, the Western, and the Eastern Palace. The Northern Palace has been deserted since the Queen was murdered there in 1895. Her apartments, which are still shown, consist of a series of tiny rooms, each eight feet square, and communicating with each other by means of sliding wall-panels. The palace servant who shows you round points out what he describes as the " Queen's dead room," and, recalling the accounts one has heard of the murder, imagination peoples these tiny rooms and narrow passages with the terrified forms of the Queen's ladies and attendants. It all took place in the pale dawn of a summer's morning, and when the sun rose the body of the Queen was burning on a hastily-erected funeral-pyre in the palace gardens. Her last words, spoken to one of the faithful attendants who refused to desert her, were an inquiry

The Sights of Seoul

whether all was well with her dearly-loved son, the Crown Prince, the present Emperor of Korea.

The last Queen of Korea (for it was some years after her death that the "Hermit Kingdom" was changed into an Empire) seems to have been one of those people who are in advance of the times they live in. Those who knew her intimately say that she loved her people, and saw with wonderful clearness what reforms were needed to make them prosperous and happy. Handicapped by the traditionally subordinate position accorded to women in her country, and without the abnormally strong will and the entire unscrupulousness of the Chinese Empress, she had few opportunities of making herself felt in public affairs during the ten short years of her reign. But to those who jealously watched Korea, endeavouring to check every effort that might make for her strength and prosperity, the Queen, as a possible power behind the throne, was an obstacle which they were determined to remove out of their way.

Her sudden and violent death left her spouse in a pitiable condition of nervousness. Night after night he begged for, and obtained, the presence of some foreigner in the palace, now become for him an abode of dread and terror; and one day the Russian Minister utilized these fears to obtain a diplomatic victory. He persuaded the Emperor to take refuge in the Russian Legation, whither he was secretly conveyed in a chair belonging to one of the Court ladies. Thus he remained under Russian protection until the pressure brought to bear on the matter by the representatives of all the interested Powers at length induced him to put himself under their combined care. But he could never reconcile himself to the royal dwelling which had been the scene of the tragedy recounted above, and so the palace where the Court at present resides was built in the neighbourhood, and, indeed, practically surrounded by the foreign Legations.

The Eastern Palace, the oldest in Seoul, has been deserted since the day, some fifty or sixty years ago, that the then King of Korea, looking forth from one of the windows, saw, or imagined that he saw, a serpent fall from one of the royal roofs. Those wise men who were versed in these things pronounced this to be an omen of dire import, and a warning that His Majesty should depart without delay. There are also the remains of

The Sights of Seoul

the Mulberry Palace, of which only one pavilion is standing at the present day. It is now used as a meeting-place for those who practise the ancient art of archery.

Another of the sights of Seoul is the Great Bell mentioned already. Its voice is never heard, but it was, one is told, of surpassing sweetness. The story runs that the craftsman to whom was intrusted the casting of the metal failed twice in producing the bell without a flaw. The third time his daughter, determined to save her father's credit, and perhaps his life (for the bell was a royal order, and monarchs were not patient in those far-off days), cast herself into the molten mass. A perfect bell was the result, the beauty of whose tone was, according to the fable, the result of the love and self-sacrifice which had gone to its making.

Amongst the "lions" of Seoul must also be counted the pagoda—a beautiful piece of carving in white marble, supposed to be of Chinese origin. It occupies a piece of ground which has lately been turned into a public garden, and where the German-trained royal band plays every afternoon.

From the description I have given, you will

Korea

perceive that there is not much to be seen in Seoul. The real charm and interest of the city lies in the motley life as you see it day after day in the streets. "An Englishman's house is his castle," and there he loves to shut himself in, with his family and a few friends, and to celebrate the family fêtes and to mourn the family griefs; but the Oriental allows you to share in all this. You see him as he mourns and weeps aloud for his dead father, and as he gaily escorts his newly-married son to the latter's new home. You can also see him bargaining, dictating his letters to the professional scribe, who sits by the roadside, consulting the doctor or the soothsayer, or having his teeth drawn.

CHAPTER XIII

THE FOUR ESTATES OF THE REALM

IN Korea there are four distinct classes of society. They are as follows: The Royal Family, the nobles, the farmers, the traders and artisans. The present Royal Family is descended, although not directly, from Ni Taijo, who became King of Korea in 1368. The Emperor is an absolute monarch, with power of life and death over his subjects. His person is sacred—so much so that a King of Korea has died from an abscess which his doctor was not permitted to lance. For this reason, also, the portrait of the ruler is not allowed to appear on the coins of the realm, which must pass from hand to hand, and may frequently be dishonoured by falling into the dust.

The nobility of Korea is very powerful, exercising great influence in the government of the country. Most of the high offices of the State are filled by members of the aristocracy. Although the Chinese system of giving preferment

Korea

to the successful candidates in the Government examinations exists, for the students have to show a thorough acquaintance with Chinese philosophy and ethics, yet this system is modified by the fact that State employment is regarded as the only possible career for the son of a noble. As most of the nobles are very poor, they take care to keep the State appointments among themselves. In China things are arranged quite differently, for there the poorest boy may, by dint of study and perseverance, rise to the highest post.

There is one thing, however, in which Korea resembles the Celestial Empire, and that is in the amount of " squeeze-pidgin " which is carried on. All money, from the State revenue to the pay of the poorest coolie, pays its toll to every hand through which it passes on its way to the rightful recipient. This system leads naturally to much injustice and oppression, and for the poor man there is no redress.

The farmers also suffer much from the tax-collectors, who are sent out by the Government. It is of no advantage to them to improve their land and increase their stock. This only means that they will have to give up more to the greedy officials who come to them " in the name of the

The Four Estates of the Realm

Emperor." " It is better for us," they say, " to make just enough to live on, for that they must leave us." At best their life is a hard and miserable one. In spring they drive their rough wooden ploughs through the rice-fields, wading knee-deep in slimy water. Later the melon-gardens have to be guarded night and day from possible thieves. In the winter the mountainsides have to be searched for sticks and leaves for the *kang*, that he and his family may not die of cold in their wretched hovel.

The fourth class of Korean society comprises all traders and craftsmen, and includes, besides, the followers of the " vile callings "—*i.e.*, the butcher, the boatman, and the gaoler, the letter-carrier and the sorceress. The craftsmen of Korea, although their forebears gave to Japan the skill and knowledge which were the beginning of the exquisite productions of that country, are now chiefly remarkable for the uniform mediocrity of their work. One reason for this is, naturally, the extreme poverty of the people in general, which forbids their spending money on anything beyond the actual necessities of life. Another is the fact that almost every household is, to a great extent, self-supplying. All Korean women can

Korea

spin and weave, and many of them do the tailoring and shoemaking for the family; while the men manufacture the harness for the beasts, the house furniture, and the rude implements of the farm. All these articles are, therefore, in little demand, and those who manufacture them are forced to sell at so small a profit that they cannot afford to spend much time over them. But even in the making of pottery, which is entirely in the hands of the professional worker, there is displayed none of that feeling for design and appropriate ornament which makes even the most ordinary specimens from China or Japan such a joy to every lover of the beautiful. The usual complaint of the tourist in Korea is that there is " nothing to buy."

CHAPTER XIV

A ROYAL PROCESSION

THE Emperor very seldom leaves his palace. When he does so, he likes to impress his subjects with the magnificence of the procession which accompanies him. I was lucky enough to be in Seoul on a special occasion, when His Majesty went out to worship at the tomb of the Queen. A certain number of the Europeans then in Seoul had been invited to lunch in a pavilion not very far from the tomb, and to witness the august arrival there. The month was October, and the day a glorious one—the sort of day we in England call "a real autumn day," but of which we seldom get more than three or four during that season. In Korea, on the contrary, you can, as soon as the summer rains are over, count on having three months of almost unbroken sunshine and clear, bracing air.

On this particular day the electric tramway conveyed us through the east gate of the city, and to the beautiful spot, three miles beyond it, where the Queen's tomb is situated. The tomb itself is a hideous structure, quite devoid of charm. It was erected over all that remained of the royal victim, after her body had been burned by her murderers in the palace-garden. The pious researches of her attendants on the following day could only discover the bone of one finger.

Arrived at our destination, we were received by two of the palace interpreters, and were shortly afterwards seated at a well-spread luncheon-table, in one of the adjacent pavilions. Lunch was a very cheery meal, but of what it was composed I remember nothing, except that there was champagne, and a cake with very hard pink icing, and several plates piled high with English sweets.

When it was over, we strolled out to see if there were any signs of the procession. We climbed one of the small adjacent hills, whose rocky sides were all covered with a dwarf Virginia creeper, with leaves of scarlet and gold. Standing on the crest of the hill, we could see the royal pageant winding through the valley below. Conspicuous in the brilliant sunshine was the golden

A Royal Procession

palanquin of the Emperor and the yellow umbrella which is always carried before him. As the procession drew near, we saw that it was headed by a crowd of palace servants, in red and yellow, some of whom carried curiously embroidered banners. Next came the *yangbans*, or nobles, on horseback. As they approached each one dismounted stiffly from his gaily-decorated steed, and, supported on either side by a servant, waddled solemnly towards the great gate of the tomb, in all the affected helplessness of a Korean grandee. Each was attired in a voluminous robe of madder brown, with crimson sleeves, a blue sash, knotted at the side, and a blue felt hat, ornamented with a bunch of peacock's feathers, and a horse's tail dyed scarlet, which hung down behind. Each carried, as a sign of official rank, a short polished baton, decorated with blue ribbons.

Then we heard a curious wailing cry, which announced the coming of His Imperial Highness. The Emperor sat in his golden palanquin, his blue robe embroidered with the royal dragons, symbols of might and power. He returned our salutations with bows and smiles, for he was always really pleased to see foreigners, when they

Korea

did not come to extort or to demand anything from him. The Crown Prince, in his crimson palanquin, followed his father, and to him succeeded a motley crowd of courtiers dressed in all the colours of the rainbow. The chief personages of the procession then vanished into one of the pavilions. Reappearing in the white dress of mourners, they passed within the gate of the tomb.

It was now four o'clock in the afternoon, and it was getting very chilly. We began to think, with a good deal of longing, of the cheery fires which awaited us at home; but the guests of royalty, although in some respects so fortunate, must not depart without leave. We were even afraid that, as sometimes happened on these occasions, the Emperor might invite us to make part of the returning procession. Our fears were, however, relieved by a message dispensing with our further attendance—an instance of Imperial consideration which won our heartfelt gratitude.

CHAPTER XV

CONCERNING SEOUL

IT was a beautiful summer evening when I took my first walk through Seoul. The principal street of the city is always thronged, chiefly with idle men, dressed in the height of Korean fashion, and it may be called the Piccadilly of Seoul. These men are chiefly the younger sons of nobles and landowners, who have failed to obtain any official post, and who, in accordance with Korean ideas, can take up no other work. Proudly they swagger along, swinging the skirts of their gay robes, which are of green, yellow, pink, blue, and violet. Now and again, with much shouting from obsequious attendants, some high official is borne through the crowd in his open four-bearer chair, or, if he has come from a long distance, the shafts of his chair will be attached to the saddles of two mules, one in front and the other behind. Court dignitaries pass on pony- or donkey- back, each one clad in the official blue

Korea

robe, and firmly holding on to the handle fixed in the pommel of his saddle, while one groom leads his pony and two others on either side hold his feet in the stirrups. Chairs or palanquins, with their little sliding windows tightly closed, are borne through the crowd, carried by two men, moving at a jog-trot, which makes one feel sorry for the poor lady inside. The gentler sex is further represented by mysterious figures in long green cloaks, from the folds of which a pair of dark eyes peer curiously at us. Here and there are to be seen strange figures clothed all in dust colour. On their heads are huge domed hats, and they hold screens made of a piece of linen stretched on two sticks before their faces. These are the mourners, and, as mourning for father or mother lasts for three years, there are usually a good many of them to be seen about.

Through this varied crowd there flit the daintiest little figures imaginable. They are those of boys from ten to fourteen years old, in rose-pink robes, their foreheads bound with the band of horsehair which is worn only by married men, and, jauntily perched on their little heads, the most comical yellow straw hats, with high

Concerning Seoul

crowns. These are the boy-bridegrooms, and how proud they look as they strut along, their chins in the air! Already they have acquired the inimitable swagger of the Korean married man. Look at the little fellow over there! He has got hold of a cigarette, which he smokes in the most grown-up manner, and you can see how patronizing he is to his unmarried friend, who is probably just about his age.

While we are watching the crowd, it suddenly scatters to right and left, and you see that a long procession of laden ponies is being driven down the street. These are pack-ponies, bringing the produce of the country into Seoul, and, as quite half of the poor little animals are blind, it is well to keep out of their way. The provisions they carry will to-morrow be displayed in the various markets of the city.

The street we are now in, East Street, is the place where the grain and fruit market is held, and if you come here in the early morning, you will find everyone very busy. Down the middle of the roadway each dealer has arranged his mats and baskets, heaped with grain of various sorts, and here are would-be purchasers, driving hard bargains as they run the grain through their fingers to test its quality. All the time the excited crowd of buyers and sellers keeps up a continual shouting, for in Korea no business can be got through without much noise.

In the fruit-market, a little higher up, you will see baskets piled high with tiny pink cherries, and when autumn comes there will be golden persimmons and crimson peaches, and heaps of the prettiest little apples, with a bloom on them like that of a grape.

Down the side of the street, stand in rows the pack-ponies upon which Seoul depends for her food-supply. Wretched little animals most of them are—ewe-backed, knock-kneed, their poor backs galled by the clumsy pack-saddles; for, sad to say, the Koreans, like most Orientals, are very indifferent to the sufferings of animals.

Near one of the city gates is the vegetable and poultry market. Here, besides fowls and ducks, you can buy wild game-birds of many sorts—pheasants, bustards, partridges, quail, wild-geese. One curious thing here is that the eggs are sold, as it were, by the yard, being all tied together in rows with straw rope. As to vegetables, you can

SERVANTS OF THE EMPEROR

Concerning Seoul

get potatoes, cabbages, various sorts of pumpkins, and vegetable-marrows, beans, and aubergines. The meat-market, close by, is not a pleasant place to visit, as the Koreans have a way of hacking up the carcasses of animals which would shock an English butcher.

CHAPTER XVI

THE HISTORY OF CHRISTIANITY IN KOREA

THE first Christians who ever set foot in Korea were Japanese converts, who formed part of the Emperor Hideyoshi's invading army; but, so far as we can learn, not even the priests who accompanied the force made any attempt to spread the Gospel of Christ among the people of Chosen. The story of its advent is a very wonderful one. In the year 1777, on the top of a lonely mountain, a company of thoughtful and, for the most part, learned men met together. For long their hearts and minds had been filled with a great ambition to penetrate the mystery of life and death. To discover the key to this was their intense desire, and to this end they resolved to devote the long, dark winter season. The greatest intellects of all ages have occupied themselves with this problem, which was so simply and touchingly expressed by the sixth-century Northumbrian in his answer to King Eadwine: "It seems to me that our life

The History of Christianity in Korea

here is as when a bird comes in at the window from the darkness, and, flying through the lighted chamber, goes out again into the night, and we cannot tell whence he comes or whither he goes; and what we look for is a religion that will teach us this." In their mountain pagoda these patient Korean seekers after the truth consulted and disputed together. They had at their command the writings of most of the Chinese philosophers, and amongst them were several books showing forth the doctrines of Christianity. Doubtless these had been brought from Peking, where the Jesuit Fathers had for long been established.

The winter passed slowly away, and when the sun and the warm winds of spring had melted the snows, and released these self-immured prisoners, they came down the mountain-side firmly convinced that in Christ's teaching lay the true hope of salvation for men. Their great desire was for an ordained priest. An urgent appeal for one was sent to the Jesuit Bishop at Peking, but, so great were the difficulties for any foreigner in crossing the Korean frontier, that twenty years elapsed before their longing could be gratified. In spite of persecutions, the Christians in Korea increased rapidly, and were found in all grades of society.

Korea

In 1800 two daughters of the ruling house embraced the faith of the "Master of Heaven," a literal translation of the Korean name for God, and were condemned to death by poison.

In 1827 the Pope entrusted the care of the Church in Korea to the Société des Missions Étrangères. A wonderful story is told in Père Dallet's "Histoire de l'Église dans la Corée" of the efforts of Brugenière, a member of this mission, to reach the "Hermit Kingdom." Landing at Macao, the Portuguese colony, he travelled through China and Tartary, disguised as a Mandarin, often obliged to refrain from food and drink, and even from sleep, for fear of betraying his identity. Three years of hardship and exposure ended for him in death, when actually within sight of the Korean frontier. His splendid example inspired others to like efforts, and many priests succeeded in entering Korea—some across the mountains from China, others from the sea, landing secretly from fishing-boats and trading-junks. In spite of edicts and persecutions, the mission flourished. In 1866, under the Tai-ouen-koun, called the "Man of the Heart of Stone," Father of the Emperor, many hundreds of

The History of Christianity in Korea

About twelve years later the present Roman Catholic Bishop of Seoul succeeded in making his way into the Hermit Kingdom. For years he remained there in hiding. At length, when he had completely mastered the language, he went back to France, and, having gathered together a band of devoted missionaries, he returned to Korea. Some of these men are still working, and it was my privilege to meet several. The priests of the Roman Catholic Church now number between forty and fifty, and, according to their own records, the converts are about 40,000.

The mission in Korea of the Society for the Propagation of the Gospel has stations in Seoul, Chemulpo, and Kanghoa; and the Anglican Sisters have opened an orphanage in Seoul, where " famine children "—unhappily an annual crop in Korea—are taken in and cared for.

CHAPTER XVII

A MORNING WALK

DURING the " hot season," which lasts from the middle of June to the end of September, the only times when exercise can be enjoyed are in the early mornings and after sunset. A favourite walk in the neighbourhood of Seoul is one which leads you past the White Buddha, and brings you back by the Peking Pass and the Arch of Independence.

We will imagine that we are sallying forth at 6 a.m. on a peaceful summer morning, and if the mornings in Korea are not always calm, one really feels they ought to be so, for the old name of the country, " Chosen," means " Land of the Morning Calm." As we walk through the streets the town seems to be scarcely awake. There are a few country-people to be seen, who have brought in provisions for the early market. At his newly-opened house-door the Korean citizen is squatting with his long pipe, sleep not yet banished from

A Morning Walk

his heavy eyes, nor the creases of the night from his dingy white suit. Thoughts of the "daily task" which, presumably, he will be called on to perform, appear not yet to have entered his beclouded brain. In an Indian city the devout Hindu would already have concluded his devotions at the sacred shrine or on the river's bank, and would be off to his shop or counting-house. A Chinese town at this hour would be a scene of humming activity. The town-bred Korean seems to be unique in his apathetic laziness.

Passing the entrance to the North Palace, we climb the steep way to the northern gate of the city. This, although within the city walls, is a real mountain road. On the right rise the rocky sides of the hill called Nam Han, and on the left a grassy bank slopes down to a stream which is very popular as a laundry. Fragrant dew-laden roses twine across the path; the grass is studded with tiny lilac-tinted irises; the sophronaria, most graceful of shrubs, waves abroad its spikes of delicate butterfly-like blossoms.

From the north gate a rocky track leads down to a fertile valley, and here the path follows closely the course of the stream. We pass by the house of a *mutang* sorceress, against the

Korea

wall of which is a great heap of stones, raised by her half-adoring and half-fearful votaries. A little farther on is a huge boulder, the sides of which are covered with small cuplike hollows. The people tell you that if you can manage to get a pebble to stick in one of these hollows, your greatest wish, whatever it may be, is certain to be fulfilled. We next pass by two or three small farms, and the farmers, standing still to watch us go by, will probably ask with aimless curiosity: " Lady, where are you going ?" (" Pouin, oddy kao ?").

Emerging from the valley, we come to the river, and, crossing on a pathway of stones and climbing the opposite bank, we stand before the White Buddha. It is cut in low relief on the face of a huge boulder, and the figure is painted white. No one knows who carved it, how many years ago, or why it was placed in this lonely spot.

Continuing our way, and following the track, which now leads us through rice-fields, we come to the old road by which the annual Embassy passed on its way to Peking. This, with the exception of the road to Mapu, the river-port of Seoul, is the most frequented highway in the

A Morning Walk

neighbourhood of the city. Here you may see the goggled *yangban* in his travelling-chair, which is carried in this way: Two of the bearers walk close to the chair, behind and before, holding the poles in their hands, while the other two support on one shoulder, over which and under the poles a strong linen band is passed. Thus, on the foremost and hindmost bearers falls the greater part of the weight, and they constantly shift the pole from one shoulder to the other. You will also meet rude carts, with clumsy wooden wheels, filled with wood or with huge blocks of stone for building: they are drawn by great sleepy bullocks, who move at the rate of about two miles an hour; also bands of licensed pedlars, some of whom carry on their backs wooden frames covered with netting, and containing six or eight fowls of ruffled yet resigned aspect. These pedlars all belong to a guild, which is so powerful and well organized that the Government dare not interfere with them.

Passing through a narrow rocky gorge, known as the Peking Pass, we come to the hideous Arch of Independence, erected by the Japanese for the Koreans after the late war. At the same time they pulled down the old arch, under which the rulers

Korea

of Korea used formerly to await the envoys from the Chinese Emperor. Thus the suzerainty of China was tacitly declared to be at an end. Japan then attained that which she had long desired —the protectorate of Korea. This change could not fail to benefit the Koreans, who, although they have many fine qualities, have yet proved quite unable to hold their own as an independent nation : for as long as they were permitted to adhere to their ancient hermit policy they continued to exist, but only to exist, for there was neither progress nor prosperity amongst them; but once they had inevitably yielded to the demands of the Powers, and had opened their country to foreign intercourse, their inherent feebleness showed itself, and Korea became a bone of contention, pulled hither and thither by opposing claimants. Happily for her, she has now been placed under the guidance of a nation who has already made apparent her influence for good in the old land of Chosen.

CHAPTER XVIII

KOREA BECOMES PART OF THE JAPANESE EMPIRE UNDER ITS OLD NAME OF "CHOSEN"

SINCE I wrote the concluding words of the previous chapter the position of Korea has been entirely changed. She is now no longer a semi-independent State, for she has become a part of the Japanese Empire. Her people are now one with that wonderful nation, which has succeeded in absorbing Western culture and knowledge, and in applying them to her own advantage; and, what is far more important, she has not in the process lost any of the fine qualities which have always distinguished her. For, although the Japanese gentlemen now cut their hair in European fashion, and, if they are civilians, they most probably wear black coats, yet the hearts which beat beneath are as full of daring and of devoted loyalty as were ever those of the splendid old "Samurai," their ancestors, with their creed of "Better death than dishonour."

The annexation of Korea by Japan has long been with the true well-wishers of the "Hermit Kingdom" a consummation devoutly to be wished. In the old state of things, before the Japanese protectorate began, there was absolutely no hope of progress. In the hands of a ludicrously incompetent and corrupt Government things went on year after year in much the same manner—neither improving nor growing worse. Since the establishment of Japanese influence in the country numerous reforms have been carried out. Schools have been established, where modern subjects are taught in the best way. The new hospitals are furnished with all the latest improvements, and Korean women have been trained to act as nurses. Much attention has also been given to the supply of water for towns and to the improvement of existing sanitary conditions. In addition to all these tangible benefits, one feels that the spirit of energy and progress which the Japanese have brought with them into the country must have its effect in stimulating to great efforts the somewhat passive Korean. It is quite possible that this ancient

Korea Part of the Japanese Empire

people, roused at length from their long apathy, may in time give to the world great soldiers, great writers, or great painters. For many years some of the more intelligent among the younger generation of Koreans have banded themselves together, with the idea of obtaining for their countrymen greater freedom and progress. They will now have an opportunity of working to this end under the best possible teachers. The announcement that Japan intends to restore to Korea her ancient name of Chosen, or " Land of the Morning Calm," is very interesting. Those of her sons who loved her best have always in their hearts called her by this beautiful name.

Lightning Source UK Ltd.
Milton Keynes UK
UKOW05n1813010517
300285UK00010B/55/P

9 781359 221698